Creative Disruption:
7 Effective Strategies for Millennials to Lead in the Workplace

Arika J. Linton

Creative Disruption: 7 Effective Strategies for Millennials to Lead in the Workplace © 2025 by Arika J. Linton

All Rights Reserved.

No part of this book may be reproduced in any form or by any electronic or mechanical means including information storage and retrieval systems, without permission in writing from the author. The only exception is by a reviewer, who may quote short excerpts in a review.

Printed in the United States of America
First Printing: February 2025
The Scribe Tribe Publishing Group

ISBN-978-1-958436-42-4 (digital)
978-1-958436-43-1 (paperback)

Dedicated to little me. It's always been you, all you needed was to find the value of your voice!

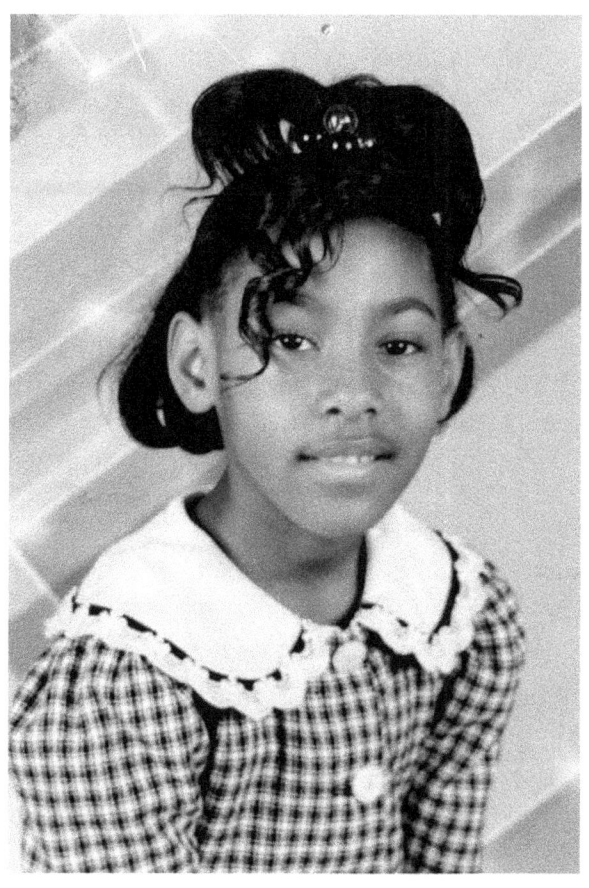

Contents

Foreword v

Introduction 1

Chapter 1: Be You, Everyone Else Is Taken 6

Chapter 2: Authenticity 8

Chapter 3: Discovering Your Voice in the Workplace 12

Chapter 4: Innovation Unlocks the Door to Freedom 14

Chapter 5: Impact 16

Chapter 6: Power of the Pivot 18

Chapter 7: High Value Employee 22

Meet the Author 24

Foreword

Being a disruptor in the workplace involves challenging the status quo, introducing new ideas, and pushing for change that can lead to improvements in how things are done. Disruptors are often seen as innovative thinkers who question existing practices, introduce new technologies or processes, and ultimately help organizations evolve in response to changing market conditions or internal inefficiencies.

Workplace disruption can be a rewarding path for those passionate about innovation, problem-solving, and driving meaningful change. However, it requires careful navigation of workplace dynamics and a willingness to embrace both success and failure as part of the process.

Creative Disruption: 7 Effective Strategies For Millennials To Lead In The Workplace has entered the chat. What you will get in these pages is a guide for innovative and authentic disruption for those looking to win in the workplace but don't quite see the path to success. This is not your average…

Millennials, who are currently in the midst of their careers, can significantly benefit from reading *Creative Disruption* as the workplace has drastically changed over the past few decades with the rise of technology, remote work, and a more diverse and globalized workforce. From the power of authenticity, finding your voice, leveraging innovation for more freedom, understanding if and when to pivot, to delivering as a high value employee, this short read is a guidebook to help millennials better understand how to navigate this modern, fast-paced environment, adapt to changes, and thrive in evolving organizational cultures.

Those who have had the pleasure of knowing Arika know her as a power broker in the City of Chicago who has impacted the landscape and those who have listened to her TEDx Talk or read her musings also know her as a genuine force in creating pathways for others through story, inspiration, and opportunity. Arika's writing mimics her work in life - empowering listeners through both resources and her lived experience.

She is transparent about her journey in finding her voice and *Creative Disruption* is necessary reading for underrepresented talent interested in success strategies for navigating the future of work. This work goes beyond the platitudes and gets tangible to really help employees determine their north star and thrive in the workforce.

Halleemah Nash
Founder, Rosecrans Ventures

Introduction

"You can run but you can't hide…" That statement sums up my life personally and professionally. I've deleted many iterations of this introduction simply because I can't believe this is happening.

Can I be honest?

I have not always been a disruptor or challenger. In fact, anyone that you ask from my younger years can confirm this statement to be true. As a matter of fact, I was the kid that didn't speak up. I oftentimes brushed off things that rubbed me the wrong way until I discovered my power and voice.

As a millennial in mid-management, I've learned the value of showing up authentically and leading by example. In any professional space, it is my goal to lead with compassion, encourage tenacity, and provide opportunities for innovation and a growth mindset amongst team members. In my role as a director of secondary success at OneGoal, a nonprofit organization in Illinois, it is my job to advocate and empower educators to find culturally responsive and organic solutions that aid student success as they embark on their next journey graduating from high school. I collaborate with external and internal stakeholders to curate messaging and curriculum that engages our students in under resourced communities. This undertaking requires having my pulse on the culture and engaging consistently in the most authentic way.

In the workplace, I've become a disruptor naturally. I see a thing and then I see how I can change it effectively through a creative lens. When I transitioned into the education industry in 2017, I started as a dean of students, which is typically a role with very little creativity. However, my supervisor, the principal, gave me complete autonomy to implement the approach of "conversation over consequence." Simply put, this is a strategy that allows the outcome of a student to be solved with a conversation and not suspension in hopes to change the outcome next time. I irritated a lot of people (my colleagues mostly) by not suspending students for misbehavior and instead sought out ways to change their behavior through learned experiences.

Creative Disruption

These learned experiences included high value exposure. To quote B.Lin, author of *How You See It: The Power of Perspective*, "Exposure is proof of life's possibilities." That being said, I maximized the opportunity to put a spin on the traditional role of a dean of students. I featured CEO/Founder of Mielle Organics, Monique Rodriguez, as "Principal For The Day", so that students could see a real-time millionaire who looks just like them. Throughout the school year, free haircuts, bookbags, and school supplies were given to students so that they could feel self-love and empowerment from a community that cares about them. Another staple moment was making *International Day of The Girl* a hands-on immersive experience in partnership with the hair care brand Luster's Pink. This immersive experience included a full-service nail bar for students K-8th to receive manicures, empowerment sessions from keynote speakers, dance workshops, and beauty stations which featured Luster's Pink products and hair extensions so each young lady could receive complimentary styles from licensed cosmetologists. This is still one of the most talked about experiences. I learned early on that my students strive and change through love, not suspension.

Many people would ask, "What does that have to do with being a dean of students?" My response was simple. "Nothing, if you are judging it through the lens of your lived experience." However, I was very clear on my assignment; I was there to disrupt the norm. That has pretty much been the sum of my career the last seven years. Once I realized my power was innovation through disruption and my success would be found in my authenticity, I discovered my secret sauce.

By now, you may be wondering what is Arika's purpose in sharing her experiences? I want my peers to win! I gain nothing by gatekeeping what has positioned me for success in the workplace. If you are a millennial or young creative professional, you're probably facing challenges with pivoting into a new field. Well after reading this, you will walk away with clear, actionable steps on how to land your dream job using these seven strategies.

This book is a practical guide for millennials navigating the workplace, focusing on the power of authenticity, innovation, and creative disruption. Drawing from personal and professional experiences, I share strategies for discovering one's voice, leading with purpose, and driving meaningful impact for career success.

Tag, you're it!

Chapter 1

Be You, Everyone Else Is Taken

As a millennial, it's important to understand that being an impactful leader takes time. No one starts out as an expert. I believe that over time you grow into your value and voice within the organization, but first you must seek to understand your role and function before change can exist.

Understanding who you are and what you bring to the workplace takes practice. It takes multiple iterations of trial and error moments in order to succeed. Before identifying where you want to ascend, you have to understand who you are. Who do you desire to show up as professionally? What kind of leader are you? What kind of impact do you plan to make in the workplace?

That starts with showing up as your authentic self.

When it comes to creative disruption it really boils down to the implementation of unique strategies that allow you to serve as a solutionist.

What problem are you called to solve in the workplace?

Disrupt the norm then provide the solution.

My definition of Creative Disruption can be described as: **the millennial way to fuel positive change within companies, communities, and the world at large through innovation and ideas, thus effectively impacting an organization.**

How do you do that? One word–AUTHENTICITY!

What fuels your authenticity in the workplace?

For this first exercise I need you to grab a pen and paper. Take a moment to write your mission statement for the workplace, start with defining and identifying what you see for yourself.

Do you want to discover your leadership style?

Start with your impact. Remember, it's all in the strategy. Consider putting time on a colleague's and people manager's calendar to discuss your impact and voice on your team. This can help with framing.

What you offer to your organization and team is invaluable so get rooted in what you add.

Chapter 2

Authenticity

Any role I've accepted in the last seven years has been largely connected to how I show up. The confidence and unequivocal belief in self has carried me. The God in me has been my guiding light.

The ability to package my offering and market it in a way that's invaluable to the workplace has provided me with ample opportunities to shine.

When asked how often should you bet on yourself? The answer should always be, every time!

How did I tap into my authenticity? When I stopped trying to lead like everyone I admired. You've heard the old adage, "there's a thin line between imitation and admiration."

> **Leadership requires finding your unique voice. Leaders do not mimic.**
>
> **Authenticity is the decision to act and implement the unique voice to have the best impact.**

My Life Example: When I worked at City Year Chicago as senior manager, it was authenticity that used grassroots marketing to canvas the neighborhoods we served to recruit student success coaches. It was important that I recruited student success coaches to serve with City Year that were reflective of students we served within Chicago Public Schools. One of the most unique recruitment endeavors that I led was our partnership with WNBA Champions, the Chicago Sky, to expose our brand to an audience that was deeply unfamiliar. That strategy led to that cohort having the highest enrollment for the Chicago site. I valued my add to the organization and pushed the envelope to recruit in non-traditional ways which led to the greatest impact across sites.

Arika J. Linton

Looking for opportunities to delve deeper in your leadership style and abilities? I highly recommend the _Clifton Strengths for Leaders_[1] assessment. Purchasing this assessment will allow you to understand the importance of utilizing your power to leverage authenticity in the workplace. I am a strong advocate for this assessment because it empowers us as millennials to learn more about our strengths and how they allow us to fulfill our potential. In short, take this assessment, now!

---

[1] https://store.gallup.com/p/en-us/15310/cliftonstrengths-for-leaders?c=1

Chapter 3

Discovering Your Voice in the Workplace

What is the value of your voice in the workplace? I have learned through experience that your voice is only as strong as your results. People will not listen to a person if they cannot track your measurable success.

I have found that people have often labeled us millennials as the "talkative generation," meaning that we post an idea online before we have even figured out the plan of action. (I have been guilty of this.) Wanting people to keep up with us doesn't always equate to success, but rather only generates movement. Movement is not success. Success in the workplace can be identified as sustainable and impactful growth. The question you should be asking yourself is what role did I play in the growth through action? How did my presence move my organization forward?

I equate voice to growth and development. I have found that the most practical way to find your authentic voice is by putting in the work. What does your effectiveness and efficiency say about you?

> **A large part of collaboration is voice. It is through teamwork that people begin to validate your working style, your leadership ability, and if you are a talker or doer.**

The value of a talker: great secretary, great notetaker/keeper, connected.

The value of a doer: implementer, solution-oriented, detail focused.

As you can see, both have value, but one takes on more of a leadership role. Decide early on which role you want in the workplace.

Discovering your voice professionally can sometimes cause friction with who you are and who you want to become.

> **For this chapter, I want you to jot down 3 people you admire in the workplace and why? What is their impact and why do you look to them for admiration as a leader? Now, what makes YOU different? As a leader, it is your difference that will propel you, not your likeness.**

Cheers to finding the beauty of your voice!

Chapter 4

Innovation Unlocks the Door to Freedom

Curating your journey takes strategy.

Your major takeaway from this chapter is simple: **Innovation leads to impact.**

Innovation is my jam. Once you've mastered your voice in the workplace and the solution you're called to solve, the next step is understanding that your innovation is connected to the implementation of your strategy. Innovation is the moving piece that solidifies your place as a leader.

Innovation lives in the details.

How does innovation in the workplace aid millennials? It helps you to understand that the power of your voice aids credibility. One can only build credibility by bridging creativity, knowledge, and the opportunity for calculated risks. At this stage in your career, it's important to assess the pros and cons of potential professional opportunities while asking yourself if they land you closer or further from your ultimate goal?

Let's be clear: Trust your gut. You've got to take a chance on yourself first.

Today, I challenge you to plan out the strategy that will unlock your innovation.

Disruption of any kind takes courage:

- Courage to value yourself
- Courage to value your voice
- Courage to value your unique skill that will ultimately enhance your role in the workplace as a whole

Chapter 5

Impact

Understanding the Who, Breaking Down the How:

The Who
Creates Access [Strategy to be Implemented]

The How
Benefits From the Access [Implements Strategy to Attain Success]

As a director of secondary success, my senior director always stresses the importance of having a two-facing document. The purpose of the documents are to establish clarity on the deliverables; one for my team members to understand the "who" behind the implementation and one for the audience we coach to understand "how" behind the strategy. Never forget, the how oftentimes creates buy-in depending on the project or audience.

The goal should always be **clarity**. Clarity creates success. No matter your role, you must remain clear and align with the project's purpose to hit the benchmarks. Get comfortable speaking up if you feel the benchmarks are unsustainable by simply stating, "Here is where I am going to push back…" I have learned, especially in my current role as a director, advocacy plays a large part in hitting the goals. Sometimes the push back helps you frame the big picture goal above the immediate goal.

Never forget you're there to disrupt. This is not to cause chaos but to offer another lens or voice in your organization.

By now your strategy should be solid. You can use your voice to solidify your value within your organization. You have identified the innovation that will unlock your secret sauce in your industry. So the next step is to identify the positive effects on your innovation and secure your seat of influence through impact.

As the popular social media saying goes, "people lie, numbers don't!"

Chapter 6

Power of the Pivot

Don't be afraid of change. It's all in the movement. Being open to change is quite scary but it's a dance that I've grown to love. This dance requires impeccable attention to detail and self. What has become true for me is being open to ideas and new norms I hadn't considered to be a part of my professional growth. Additionally, what I hadn't considered was the effect it would have on me personally. **Pivoting carries its own unique spiritual power because you are shedding one version or layer to embrace another.**

I'd like to consider myself a master pivoter. Like all the chapters in this book, it takes one key component...STRATEGY. I have lived many lives (titles) which included being a freelance producer, social media and digital content manager, journalist, and educator. However, when I became a mother, I knew I wanted to lean into a career that allows flexibility, personal and professional growth.

Pivoting takes practice and is trial and error work. Being open to the consistency of change is nerve-wracking because for some of us it's right at the moment of comfort that the dance starts right back up again.

Trust Your Instincts for Career Growth

1. Recognize When It's Time to Move On

- Pay attention to your inner voice. Often, we know when a role or organization no longer aligns with our goals or values.
- Reflect on your career satisfaction. Are you growing, challenged, and fulfilled? If not, it might be time to explore new opportunities.

2. Have Career Conversations with Your Manager

- Approach your manager with a focus on your long-term professional success.
- Be transparent about your aspirations and seek feedback on how your current role can support your goals.
- Use these conversations to identify growth opportunities within the organization.

3. Map Out Your Big Picture

- Envision the highest level of success you aim to achieve outside your current organization.

- Assess how your current role or company contributes to your ultimate goals.
- Identify gaps and create a plan to bridge them, whether through new skills, experiences, or networks.

4. Evaluate Your Company's Commitment to Development

- Research professional development opportunities offered by your organization, such as fellowships, certifications, or leadership programs.
- Take advantage of these resources to enhance your skills and prepare for future roles.
- If opportunities are lacking, consider whether your organization aligns with your career growth needs.

Key Takeaways:

- Trust your instincts and listen to your inner guidance.
- Proactively engage in career development conversations.
- Align your current role with your long-term vision.

- Leverage or seek out professional development opportunities.

Eventually, change hits us all. It's just a matter of time. Get comfortable in the pivot!

Chapter 7

High Value Employee

If you've made it to this chapter, it's time you stepped into the acceptance that you are IT! This is your moment to actualize your strategy and ensure you're leading the next workplace conversation on value and growth mindset. **Acceptance looks like: I have something to offer and here's how my creative disruption aided in the big picture goal for this organization.** This should always mirror your core competencies and scorecard.

Additionally, this conversation should be rooted in how you as the employee (project manager, team leader, team member) navigated the sticky moments with insightful strategies and plans that aided in attaining the benchmarks and goals for the organization. Remember, this is not a one size fits all method. Be prepared to lean into vulnerability and model your adaptability. Your takeaways as a high value employee will leave your audience with the importance of how to pivot under pressure when a goal set may be unsustainable, or how to empower a team to achieve beyond the benchmarks (depending on your expertise).

> 💡 **Tip: Ask your senior manager how you can live up to "exceeding expectations" on your scorecard. This could be the strategy that answers that question.**
>
> **It is at this moment, you back up disruption with innovation to deliver under pressure, which is when your team and senior leaders begin to frame what kind of leader you are.**

I believe you are now ready for the necessary conversations on career development and you've identified your lane of creative disruption through the implementation of these seven strategies.

Before you leave, please answer the following two questions:

1. What does success in the workplace look like for me?
2. How do I embody workplace values at this stage of my career?

Again, tag, you're it! :)

Meet the Author

Arika J. Linton, M.A. is an award-winning nonprofit, education, and media TEDx speaker from Chicago, Illinois. Primarily known for her authenticity, innovation, and impact in the workplace. As a people-first leader she lives to create connection and access for her community.

www.ingramcontent.com/pod-product-compliance
Lightning Source LLC
Chambersburg PA
CBHW070050070426
42449CB00012BA/3214